# URUGUAY

## in pictures

*Montevideo*

By NATHAN A. HAVERSTOCK
and JOHN P. HOOVER,
THE LATIN AMERICAN SERVICE

STERLING PUBLISHING CO., INC. NEW YORK

Oak Tree Press Co., Ltd. London & Sydney

# VISUAL GEOGRAPHY SERIES

Afghanistan
Alaska
Argentina
Australia
Austria
Belgium and Luxembourg
Berlin—East and West
Bolivia
Brazil
Bulgaria
Canada
The Caribbean (English-
  Speaking Islands)
Ceylon (Sri Lanka)
Chile
China
Colombia
Costa Rica
Cuba
Czechoslovakia
Denmark
Ecuador
Egypt
El Salvador
England

Ethiopia
Fiji
Finland
France
French Canada
Ghana
Greece
Greenland
Guatemala
Haiti
Hawaii
Holland
Honduras
Hong Kong
Hungary
Iceland
India
Indonesia
Iran
Iraq
Ireland
Islands of the
  Mediterranean
Israel
Italy

Jamaica
Japan
Jordan
Kenya
Korea
Kuwait
Lebanon
Liberia
Madagascar (Malagasy)
Malawi
Malaysia and Singapore
Mexico
Morocco
Nepal
New Zealand
Nicaragua
Norway
Pakistan and Bangladesh
Panama and the Canal
  Zone
Peru
The Philippines
Poland
Portugal
Puerto Rico

Rhodesia
Rumania
Russia
Saudi Arabia
Scotland
Senegal
South Africa
Spain
Surinam
Sweden
Switzerland
Tahiti and the
  French Islands of
  the Pacific
Taiwan
Tanzania
Thailand
Tunisia
Turkey
Uruguay
The U.S.A.
Venezuela
Wales
West Germany
Yugoslavia

## PICTURE CREDITS

The publishers wish to thank the following for their co-operation in furnishing photographs: Nathan A. Haverstock and John A. Hoover, The Latin American Service, Washington, D.C.; Organization of American States, Washington, D.C.; United Nations, New York; Uruguayan Mission to the United Nations, New York; Uruguayan National Office of Tourism; Varig Airlines; and World Health Organization, New York.

# CONTENTS

## URUGUAY

— International boundary
⊙ National capital
— Road
┼┼┼┼ Rail

| | 20 | | 40 Miles |
| 0 | 20 | 40 | Kilometres |

BRAZIL

Monte
Caseros
Bella
Unión
Artigas
Quaraí
Santana do
Livramento
Belén
Rivera

ARGENTINA

Río Arapey Grande

Concordia
Salto

BRAZIL

Río Daymán
Tacuarembó
Aceguá

Río Tacuarembó

C U C H I L L A   d e   H A E D O

Río Queguay Grande
Tres
Arboles
Paysandú

Melo
Pan American

Río Yaguarón

Río Negro

Río Branco
Jaguarão

Concepción
del
Uruguay

Young

Paso
de los
Toros
Dam

EMBALSE DEL
RÍO NEGRO

Río Tacuarí

Santa Clara

Río Negro

Río Yi
Durazno

Sarandí
del Yi

Treinta y Tres
Cebollatí

Fray
Bentos
Mercedes

Dolores

Río San Salvador
Cardona

Trinidad

José Pedro
Varela

C U C H I L L A   G R A N D E

Río Cebollatí

Chuy

Carmelo

Florida

Uruguay

ISLA MARTÍN
GARCÍA
(Claimed by
Argentina and
Uruguay)
Colonia

San
José

Río Santa Lucía
Lucía

Minas

Rocha

ATLANTIC
OCEAN

Pan American Highway

Juan L.
Lacaze

Santa
Lucía
Canelones
Las
Piedras
Pando

La Paloma

BUENOS
AIRES

La
Plata

RÍO DE LA PLATA

MONTEVIDEO

Maldonado
Punta del Este

ARGENTINA

BOUNDARY REPRESENTATION IS
NOT NECESSARILY AUTHORITATIVE

*Uruguay is blessed with much level land, well suited to the cultivation of grains to feed both people and the nation's all-important livestock. Seen here is a vast wheat field after the grain has been cut and stacked.*

# I. THE LAND

URUGUAY, the smallest independent nation of South America, with only 72,000 square miles (187,200 sq. km.) of land, is somewhat larger than North Dakota, and larger than Ireland, Scotland and Wales combined.

Officially, the small nation is called *La República Oriental del Uruguay* ("The Eastern Republic of Uruguay") because it lies on the eastern bank of the Uruguay River. For 270 miles (432 km.) this river determines the boundary between Uruguay and Argentina, before it empties into the broad estuary called the Río de la Plata (literally the River Silver)— where fresh and ocean salt waters commingle. The estuary itself forms Uruguay's southern boundary for 235 miles (376 km.).

Uruguay's location on such a useful waterway as the Río de la Plata system is an immense advantage. Big ocean-going vessels can make their way up the estuary to unload their cargoes in the port of Montevideo, Uruguay's capital and most important city.

On the southeast, Uruguay has 120 miles (192 km.) of Atlantic coastline with fine

*From Uruguay's flocks of sheep come wool that is used as far away as the People's Republic of China and Scotland for weaving fabrics of superior quality.*

beaches, peaceful lagoons, and wind-swept dunes. To complete the circuit of Uruguay's boundaries, there remains only the nation's northeastern frontier with Brazil, which is formed in part by the Cuareim and Yaguarón Rivers, and in part by low-lying hills, ridges, and a large lake.

## TOPOGRAPHY

Fertile and rolling grasslands are the dominant feature of Uruguay's landscape—prosperous cattle ranges and crop lands which provide a welcome transition between the hot and humid *pampas*, or "plains," of northern Argentina and the subtropical uplands and plateaus of southern Brazil. There is a somewhat less humid extension of the *pampa* itself in Uruguay, a fertile, deep-soiled and level strip of land where cattle thrive, in the southeastern quarter of the country. The *pampa* merges with a wide coastal plain that extends east from Montevideo to Maldonado, and then north to the Brazilian border.

The interior of Uruguay is mainly an area of gently rolling grasslands on which meat and wool, the nation's two most important products are produced. The even sweep of the land is interrupted at two points by hilly ridges, the Cuchilla de Haedo in the northwest and the Cuchilla Grande which extends from near Montevideo northeast to the Brazilian border. Neither of these ridges reaches an elevation of

*In Uruguay, the flatness of the land makes it easy to build roads. Here a stretch between Paysandú and Tacuarembo is being paved.*

more than 1,500 to 2,000 feet (450 to 600 metres), but both have rugged crests formed by weathered outcroppings of the granite which underlies the soils of the country's eastern and southern zones.

From the Cuchilla Grande, the terrain slopes gradually westward to the Uruguay River. The northwestern corner of the country is an extension of the southernmost portion of Brazil's Parana Plateau—where, in unrecorded past ages, dark flows of lava covered over the basic granite. In Uruguay, these volcanic intrusions are set off from the adjoining lands by *cuestas*, or sharp cliffs, whose tops are flat and whose sides are steep and angular.

## RIVERS AND LAGOONS

The rivers of Uruguay are numerous and important, draining the economically productive grasslands, and providing direct access to the sea for Uruguay's exports. Along their banks, narrow ribbons of forest criss-cross the country. The bottom lands of the Río Negro widen into a large expanse of forest at the point where it enters the Uruguay River. The Río Negro itself, largest of the nation's inland waterways though its source is in Brazil, divides the country in two, along a northeast-southwest axis.

In the 1940's, the Río Negro was dammed to form a centrally located, 87-mile-long (139 km.)

lake, one of the largest man-made lakes in South America. A second dam a short distance downstream has created another, though much smaller, reservoir. Both dams have major hydro-electric installations.

Uruguay's second most important river, the Yi, a tributary of the Río Negro, rises in the hills of the Cuchilla Grande, and flows for 140 miles (324 km.). Other rivers and streams having their source in the Cuchilla Grande run eastwards along shallow courses, before feeding into lagoons near the Atlantic coast or directly into the sea itself.

Most of the nation's principal rivers are navigable—the Río de la Plata as far north as Paysandú, the Uruguay River by coastal vessels as far as the falls at Salto. The Río Negro is used by coastal shipping for about 45 miles (72 km.) inland. The Cebollatí River flows into the Laguna Merín, a large body of water on the Brazilian frontier, which is navigated by small steamers that ply routes from town to town along the shore of the lake.

Coastal lagoons, some of them bodies of fresh water fed by inland rivers and streams, are common along Uruguay's Atlantic coast. A dozen or more lagoons have surface areas of from 15 to 70 square miles (39 to 182 sq. km.), and there are numerous smaller lagoons, some of them filled with brackish water, in the area.

In all, Uruguay is a compact, pear-shaped

*Largest of the coastal lagoons is the Laguna Merín (called Mirim by the Brazilians), which forms part of Uruguay's frontier with Brazil. Flooding is a problem in the winter months in the area about the lagoon, while drought is usual in the summer. To combat these conditions, Brazil and Uruguay established the Merín Lagoon Basin Development Project to carry out flood control, irrigation and crop selection schemes. These workers for the project are harvesting an experimental crop of rice.*

country. There are no natural obstacles—mountains, deserts or jungles—to hinder the development of land transportation. At its greatest width, from the northwest corner to the southeast Atlantic coast, the country measures only about 360 miles (576 km.). The most heavily travelled and commercially important highway is only about 100 miles (160 km.) long, from Colonia on the Río de la Plata across from Buenos Aires, the Argentine capital, to Montevideo.

## CLIMATE

Uruguay's character as a land of transition is clearly evident in climate and vegetation. Consistent with the gentle "feel" of the countryside, the climate is mild and equable and without great extremes of temperature, partly owing to the moderating effect of the almost constant ocean breezes. About one-third of the days are sunny, though there is often considerable humidity, especially during the midwinter months of July and August (Uruguay is in the southern hemisphere).

Seasonal variations in temperature are modest. Winter temperatures range around 57° to 60°F. (14° to 15°C.), and, on infrequent occasions, they may drop briefly as low as the mid-20's F. (—4°C.), though without danger of snow.

Summer temperatures average about 75°F. (24°C.). But as mild as Uruguay's weather is in the summer, frequent and highly unpredictable changes can occur—a warm sunny afternoon can

*Water supply experts take readings at a meteorological station in the department (province) of Treinte y Tres. The department and its chief town are named for a band of 33 Uruguayan patriots. In the background are some of Uruguay's sparse woodlands.*

be interrupted by looming clouds and cold winds blown up from the south, bringing with them a sharp drop in temperature.

Montevideo receives about 40 inches (100 cm.) of rainfall a year, while about 50 inches (125 cm.) fall in the north, an amount which decreases somewhat in volume moving inland from the coast. Though the volume of Uruguay's rainfall is dependable, the nation's ranchers and livestock raisers anxiously watch the skies, hoping that the rain will fall when they need it. Normally, rain falls most frequently in the winter, though the heaviest storms occur in the autumn, and summer thunderstorms are common.

Uruguay has the distinction of being the only Latin American country which lies wholly outside of the tropics. Its location within the temperate zone has played an important rôle in shaping the economy and the character of both Uruguay and its people.

## GRASSLANDS AND FORESTS

Only 3 per cent of Uruguay is covered with native forests; most of the country has grazing lands suited to all kinds of livestock. Because of their importance to the Uruguayan economy,

some of the country's grasslands have been replanted in imported grasses of higher nutrient value as feed for animals.

But whether the grasses are native or imported, in the spring the rural landscape of Uruguay boasts an abundance of native wildflowers. The flowers of a native species of verbena often give a lavender cast to wide areas of the grasslands. It was the verbena, with its showy clusters of flowers, which inspired the English writer and naturalist, W. H. Hudson, to call his widely read work *The Purple Land.*

Uruguay has comparatively few kinds of trees, compared with heavily forested Brazil to the north. The trees of Uruguay are similar to others of the temperate zone, except in the far northwest of the country where forest growth is thick and dense, and tropical orchids cling to trunk and branch.

Among the trees native to the country are willows, acacias, myrtle, and laurel. There is some *lignum vitae*, a prized hardwood, and *quebracho*, whose bark is used in tanning leather. Several temperate-zone trees, not native to Uruguay, have been introduced and adapted to their environment. Poplars and eucalyptus (the latter introduced from Australia) line roadways and surround ranchers' homes.

**9**

*These seals on Lobos Island have been skinned for their valuable furs. The Uruguayan government carefully regulates this industry, in order to preserve the animals.*

Pines have been planted behind the Atlantic beaches, to help stabilize soils and prevent sand dunes from marching inland.

A whole range of fruit and nut trees has been introduced and proved of commercial value. These include peach, pear and apple trees, and various kinds of citrus fruits—oranges, lemons and grapefruit—as well as olive, almond, date, and banana trees. There are scattered tropical palms at Rocha, in southeast Uruguay, which extend in a belt across the country, marking some say, an aboriginal trade route dating from before the time of Columbus.

Easily the most striking tree is the *ombu*, whose ungainly thick trunk is depicted in early prints and paintings of Uruguay. Though the huge trunks of this tree are too pulpy to be of use in construction or as fuel, the leaves provide a welcome shade in areas devoid of other trees—and the *ombu* itself has become prominent in Uruguayan folklore.

## WILDLIFE

Uruguay is poor in four-footed animal life. Of the animals once native to the country—including pumas (mountain lions), jaguars and wildcats—most have long since been hunted to extinction, though deer, foxes and the *carpincho*, a South American water hog, are occasionally seen. The *mulita*, a small armadillo, survives in the northern hills, and the *nutria*, an aquatic rodent with a beaver-like fur, is commercially valuable.

Fur-bearing seals, whose hides are highly prized, inhabit the Isla de Lobos, a rocky island off the Atlantic coast near Punta del Este. The island boasts the southern hemisphere's most important seal rookery, or breeding ground, a sanctuary strictly controlled and protected by Uruguayan authorities.

Uruguay is rich in birdlife of incredible variety. Flightless Antarctic penguins reach

Uruguayan beaches by swimming the cold currents of water that circulate north from polar regions. The equally flightless rhea, or South American ostrich, runs with giant strides across the nation's open plains. Years ago, ostrich plumes were a significant Uruguayan export, shipped overseas to decorate fashionable ladies' hats.

Ocean birds are plentiful, as well as marsh and wading birds—including various kinds of snipe and plovers. Inland, parakeets are common, and the open lands and pastures abound with small quail-like partridges, and less numerous prairie hens, both of which are still widely hunted. Also hunted are numerous doves. A bird that attracts the traveller's attention is the ovenbird, which builds mud nests on the tops of fence posts and telegraph poles. Another striking native bird is the crow-sized *teruteru*, whose name is derived from its cry—a bird with dramatic black-and-white bands and a sharp spur on the leading edge of each wing.

Whatever its failings as a source of sport for the hunter, Uruguay is a fisherman's paradise, the waters of its southeastern coast being one of the world's major fishing grounds. Most numerous among the species found in its ocean waters are black bass, mackerel, tuna, hake, mullet, sole, whiting and anchovy. On its beaches are jetties, from which surf-fishermen cast for bluefish, weakfish and drum (so called because it makes a drumming noise).

Uruguay's rivers offer the *dorado* (literally "the golden one"), a salmon-like fish which averages 30 pounds (14 kilos) in weight and may reach 60 (27 kilos). Anglers converge on Paysandú each year to vie with one another in trying to catch one of these fighting furies. Other fresh-water fish include the *pejerrey, pacu, tararira,* and *surubi*—remotely akin to the more familiar perch and bass. The Santa Lucia River, near Montevideo, has the highly prized *criolla,* a delicious food fish which runs in weight up to 70 pounds (32 kilos).

*The seals seen here are "surplus" males, that is those who lost out in the scramble for mates, and who show their frustration by roaring and gnashing their teeth.*

*Beyond the city limits, there are vast expanses of pasture land on which to graze the cattle which provide Uruguay and foreign markets with top quality beef.*

## NATURAL RESOURCES

Uruguay has neither coal nor petroleum in appreciable quantities. The lack of these sources of energy has held back the development of industry.

Recently an important discovery of iron ore of fairly high grade was made in the central part of the country. Uruguay also has some manganese, copper, lead, and gold—but not enough of any of them to provide the basis for a mining industry.

*When it was constructed, the Palacio Salvo Hotel was Montevideo's pride—but it has long since been outstripped by modern hotels. Now converted for use as office space and for apartments, it still remains one of the city's landmarks.*

*Montevideo's waterfront is composed of a string of beaches, flanked by a highway called the Rambla. The area in the foreground is the Playa (beach) Ramírez.*

The nation does, however, have numerous marble quarries, and the beautiful stone of many hues and textures is used both at home and abroad in fine construction. Uruguay also exports some granite, limestone, talc and sand.

Unquestionably, Uruguay's principal physical resource is the black, potash-rich soil on which more than 8,000,000 head of cattle and nearly 22,000,000 sheep graze. Nearly 80 per cent of the entire nation is given over to pasture land, with an additional 10 per cent devoted to the cultivation of temperate-zone crops. Uruguay can boast that nearly all of its land area is put to productive use.

## CITIES AND TOWNS

Uruguay is the most heavily urbanized country in South America, which is not surprising, considering that about half the population lives in the metropolitan area of Montevideo—a delightful city. The capital's downtown section boasts a main thoroughfare, lined with intriguing old buildings, few of them more than a dozen floors in height. The side streets are mostly given over to shops and business establishments of modest scale.

The old port district of Montevideo has narrow streets, fine old colonial houses and

*The Carrasco Hotel and Casino is a 1920's landmark at Carrasco, one of Montevideo's most fashionable suburbs.*

*Montevideo's oldest and largest park, El Prado, is famous for its zoo, museums, gardens, fountains and artificial lakes, one of which is seen here.*

office buildings—some of them in the process of restoration. The old market, a hugh iron-framed edifice, is crammed with fresh bread and fish, delicious cheeses, sausages and meats of all kinds. Inside the market, shoppers observe such agreeable customs as drinking sweet and sour wine, chilled and mixed in a glass in equal proportions.

Further uptown, in the business district, a marked Italian feeling pervades the restaurants and shops. Arcades, lined with artfully decorated show windows meander through several down-

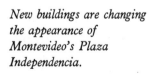

*New buildings are changing the appearance of Montevideo's Plaza Independencia.*

*At Punta del Este, bathers retreat to a shady terrace for lunch.*

town blocks. Up above, at balcony level, are tea shops and restaurants where shoppers can rest their feet and watch the activities down below.

The side streets of the capital city are rich in beef restaurants, where choice cuts are cooked to the customer's specifications over glowing charcoal hearths, along with some of the finest seafood restaurants on the continent. In all, Montevideo has a pleasant air—the supermarket, the huge department store, the sprawling traffic jams and smog of other cities have yet to arrive in Montevideo, though they may be just over the horizon.

The city itself boasts numerous and attractive parks and open spaces. It is largely free of ghettoes, in part because Uruguayans tend to have small families. The national population has remained fairly stable in size through most of this century.

No other cities in Uruguay are even remotely comparable to Montevideo, though special mention should be made of Punta del Este, the country's leading pleasure resort. Located on the Atlantic coast, a little more than an hour by car from Montevideo, it is a matter of national pride that Punta del Este has served as a conference site for major inter-American meetings in

*Rivera in Uruguay and Livramento in Brazil are actually a single town. The border follows the street above—the buildings on the left are in Uruguay.*

*Rivera, the hub of a region that produces sheep, cattle, fruit, cotton and tobacco, is connected by rail with both Montevideo and the Brazilian city of São Paulo.*

recent years—including a gathering of 19 presidents a few years ago, including the President of the United States.

Paysandú and Salto, though important as secondary ports, have only about 60,000 people each. Mercedes and Rivera, inland towns of some business importance, have 34,000 and 22,000 respectively. Other towns of note include Fray Bentos, a meat-packing hub, with 14,000; Canelones, a suburban extension of the capital, 10,000; and Maldonado, on the Atlantic coast, 6,000, a picturesque colonial town that was once a pirate stronghold.

The rural towns and villages of Uruguay, in contrast with Montevideo, are peaceful places, existing mainly for functional reasons, as supply depots for the outlying ranches and farms. Rural towns are located on good roads, emanating out from the capital, like the blades of a fan, with few paved lateral roads. The commerce of the countryside is thus very much oriented toward Montevideo and its port.

*Montevideo appeared this way shortly after its founding in 1726.*

# 2. THE HISTORY

WITHOUT GOLD, silver, or precious stones to attract greedy Spanish eyes, the territory of modern Uruguay was at first largely unmolested by Spain's New World conquerors. The region's native Indian inhabitants were left to the primitive enjoyment of the wild beauty of their haunts over much of the period of Spanish colonial history. Elsewhere in the Americas, less fortunate Indians were brutalized and made to work the mines, like serfs, so that imperial Spain might shine in looted glory.

## EARLY EXPLORERS

Throughout its history, Uruguay has been somewhat removed from well travelled paths. During the 16th century, a few of the era's celebrated explorers did stop off briefly in Uruguay, while looking in vain along the Río de la Plata for a passage by water through the heart of the continent to the Pacific Ocean. The first of them, Juan de Solís, weighed anchor but a short distance from the present site of Montevideo.

Pleased with what he saw, Solís, accompanied by an armed party, put ashore, where he and his men were quickly overpowered by fierce Charrua Indians. There on the beach, the savages built fires and devoured the hapless explorer and his men—cannibal style. Of the group that landed, only the cabin boy survived, to live on among the Indians until his rescue a dozen years later.

*These idealized bronze figures in a Montevideo park are probably the only Charruas left in Uruguay.*

In 1520, Ferdinand Magellan, a Portuguese captain in the service of Spain and the first man to lead an expedition to circumnavigate the world, sailed along the south coast of Uruguay, like his predecessor, looking for a passage to the Pacific. According to popular legend, one of Magellan's lookouts, on seeing the site of the present day Uruguayan capital from the crow's nest, cried out: "Monte vide eu!" ("I see a mountain!" in Portuguese), thus giving the city its future name.

Seven years later, Sebastian Cabot, an Englishman in the service of Spain and the second in command on the earlier and ill-fated Solís expedition, returned to the Uruguayan coast to find the surviving cabin boy, now a young man. Cabot was pleased to have the lad as an interpreter to communicate with the Indians in their own tongue, and the former cabin boy was overjoyed to be rescued.

It was on this visit that Cabot gave the "Río de la Plata" its name. Whether the explorer was inspired by the silvery shimmering surface of the water or the mistaken opinion that the banks of the river were rich in silver deposits remains a question.

Little is known of Uruguay after that, for the remainder of the 16th century. Beginning in 1580, the thrones of Portugal and Spain were united for 60 years, thus eliminating this source of Old World rivalry for Uruguay's territory. The Charrua Indians were left alone, and only on infrequent occasions were obliged to repel intruders with their clubs, spears, bows and arrows, and three-thonged *bolas*, or "stone-throwers."

*The past and the present side by side—a monument to the gaucho, stands in front of the Commercial Bank Building in Montevideo.*

## MISSIONARIES AND COWBOYS

The next century, however, found the peace of the Indians permanently disrupted with the arrival of missionaries and cattlemen. Hernando Arias, first governor of nearby Paraguay, is generally credited as the one who introduced ranching into Uruguay, shipping some cattle and horses downstream and turning them loose to run wild on the territory's native pastures.

The animals thrived and multiplied rapidly on the abundant grasslands. Soon the herds of the undomesticated creatures attracted the attention of *gauchos*—cowboys—from across the Río de la Plata living in the increasingly well settled area about Buenos Aires.

The *gauchos* have since become heroic figures in the literature and folklore of the entire area, but their early forebears were a nomadic and uncouth lot. They had no settled abodes, cared nothing for land titles or the development of civilization. They preferred simply to follow the cattle herds, use their hides for clothing and, with careless abandon, slaughter the beasts when hungry.

In 1624, Jesuit and Franciscan missionaries followed the *gauchos*, not to herd cattle, but to follow the Charruas—into villages, where they could be taught productive habits and assembled as a captive audience to hear the preaching of the Gospel. The missionaries succeeded in domesticating the Indians, extending Spanish culture and influence, and enriching themselves and their orders—something that would eventually lead to their undoing.

## RIVALRY WITH PORTUGAL

By late in the 17th century, the crowns of Spain and Portugal were no longer united, and there began within the region of the Río de la Plata an intense rivalry for territory and trade. As if to defy Spanish claims, the Portuguese established a settlement at Colonia, directly across the Río de la Plata from the Spanish settlement at Buenos Aires, in 1680.

Seeing a threat to its monopoly over an increasingly profitable river trade, Spain at once

*Santa Teresa is an 18th-century fort on the Brazilian border, now restored, which the Spanish rulers of Uruguay built to resist Portuguese encroachments.*

sent troops to capture and occupy Colonia. From this incident a feud blossomed forth that was to see Spain and Portugal intermittently at odds with one another for the next century and a half—to be joined in their squabbling by Great Britain.

Far removed from the power struggles of Old World nations, the calm and fertile lands of Uruguay were gradually settled and developed. Some of the area's *estancias* or large ranches were established in the late 17th century, and the steady march of settlers, their goods piled high on ox-drawn carts, continued apace. Towns and villages sprang up at road junctions.

During the span of almost the entire 18th century, the settlement of Uruguay went forward, virtually without help or hindrance from Spain. Spain's presence was mainly represented by priests. The work of the missionaries in promoting Christianity and Spanish culture was facilitated by the lack of remote jungles or mountain fastnesses where unwilling Indians might hide, in ignorance of the Gospel.

**19**

*The "carreta," or high-wheeled pampas cart drawn by oxen and used by early settlers in Uruguay, has been memorialized in this life-size sculpture by the nation's famed artist, José Belloni, situated in Montevideo's Batlle Park.*

With Christian ways and clothes, the Indians themselves were soon absorbed in the more numerous immigrant population, the Indian proving a valuable worker on the cattle estates.

## THE FOUNDING OF MONTEVIDEO

In 1726, Montevideo was founded, soon to become the area's chief seaport, headquarters of colonial administration, and a bastion of defence against the encroachments of others, most notably the Portuguese. The capital became a lively commercial town, with its own shopkeepers, merchants, lawyers, and doctors— a sizable middle class, in fact.

As the capital's citizens came into their own, there were pressures to free the colony from the oppressive influence of the churchmen, some of whom had grown entirely too wealthy. In response to the growth of local enterprise and initiative, the Spanish crown expelled the

Jesuit fathers in 1767, a group that, it was felt, had grown too big and too successful. From that moment the Roman Catholic missions entered upon a period of decline in Uruguay, from which they never were to recover.

According to a treaty of 1750, Spain agreed to cede to Portugal control over all local Jesuit missions in Paraguay, in exchange for Spanish control of the Portuguese colony at Colonia. When Portugal did not live up to its side of the bargain, Spain seized Colonia by force, and found 27 British merchant ships riding at anchor there—forerunners of the coming century, when Great Britain would vie for dominance of the Río de la Plata.

Though Portugal regained control of Colonia in 1763, 14 years later Spain gained permanent possession of the town, and along with it enduring influence within the territory of modern Uruguay. Spain's Bourbon monarchs began at once in 1776 to tighten up administra-

20

tion within their empire. A new Viceroyalty of the Río de la Plata was created, whose military defences were strengthened.

In addition to the present-day territory of Argentina, the new Viceroyalty—with headquarters in Buenos Aires—embraced the area of modern Bolivia, Paraguay and Uruguay. Through the administrative move, Uruguay and its capital of Montevideo were reduced to a subordinate status. Uruguayans were resentful of this demotion.

Their resentment smouldered for the next two decades until, toward the end of the 18th century, Spain and England were at war. As the conflict developed, the people of Montevideo, whose star-shaped fortress guarded the sea lanes of the Río de la Plata, could see that Spain's empire was in decline. The British fleet in these parts exercised a clear-cut supremacy over the aging Spanish flotillas.

The British occupied Buenos Aires in 1807 and Montevideo in 1808—the year when Napoleon Bonaparte and his armies overran Spain, and the year when Napoleon put his own brother Joseph on the Spanish throne. Settlers in Uruguay, as elsewhere in Spanish America, were divided in their loyalties—some pledging their allegiance to Ferdinand of Spain, Spain's rightful sovereign, even though he was Napoleon's prisoner.

## JOSÉ ARTIGAS

Amid such doubts—and anger over the mismanagement of their homeland by far-off authorities in Spain—there emerged in Uruguay a leader, José Gervasio Artigas, who was to become the hero of the territory's struggle for independence. Son of a Montevideo family, Artigas had adopted the *gaucho* way of life. He had opposed the Spanish administration in Buenos Aires, especially its discrimination against Montevideo's trade. He had thought deeply about the situation of his country, and nourished his opinions on such writings as the North American Thomas Paine's *Common Sense* and *The Rights of Man*—publications considered subversive by the Spanish authorities, though Artigas had managed to secure them in Spanish translation.

In 1811, Artigas led Uruguayans to resist successfully an invasion by Portuguese troops from Brazil. By this time Artigas was in command of *gaucho* forces—guerrilla bands—that roamed the interior of the country, taking Las Piedras and laying siege to Montevideo. When, by agreement among the Spanish, the Argentines, and the Portuguese, the siege of the city was lifted, Artigas led an exodus of about 15,000 people—one-fourth of the total population—to the west bank of the Uruguay River.

*Hernando Arias, the man who first introduced horses and cattle into Uruguay, is commemorated by this statue on the Rambla, the boulevard skirting the waterfront of Montevideo.*

*The Uruguayan painter, José Luis Zorrilla de San Martín, here depicts Artigas negotiating a commercial treaty with the English.*

For two years Artigas refused the demands of Spanish authorities in Buenos Aires to submit to their control. His price, which Buenos Aires rejected in 1813, was a guarantee of complete autonomy for Uruguay. Buenos Aires troops took Montevideo in 1814, but Artigas and his *gauchos* drove them out in 1815, and declared independence. The rebels set up a federal republic patterned after the United States, and held together a large federated area, including not only the Banda Oriental but the nothern provinces of Argentina as well.

When driven out of Uruguay by new larger and stronger Portuguese forces in 1816, Artigas withdrew to the northern Argentine provinces, where he continued to oppose the Buenos Aires central government. When he was finally defeated, in 1820, he sought sanctuary in Paraguay, where he lived in poverty for 30 years. By his heroic deeds, Artigas, his admirers say, created a Uruguayan sense of nationality and laid the foundations for the country's sovereign existence.

This was no mean accomplishment, given Uruguay's geographical location, across the river from southern South America's foremost city, Buenos Aires, and south of the continent's biggest nation, Portuguese-speaking Brazil. Had it not been for Artigas, present-day Uruguay would surely have become part of either Argentina or Brazil—and most certainly not a separate country.

That Uruguay survived into nationhood at all is largely due first to the jealousies of European powers anxious to carve up for themselves as big a portion as possible of the Río de la Plata region, and secondly to the rivalry (which continues to this day) between Argentina and Brazil. Throughout its history, Uruguay has survived mainly as a buffer state, serving to limit contact between the two big nations.

Before Artigas could complete his mission, Brazil annexed the Banda Oriental and named it the "Cisplatine Province," a name in which there was more than an echo of ancient Rome. Brazilian rule was mild enough, but the Uruguayans' newfound pride suffered. In 1825, a group of Uruguayan exiles living in Buenos Aires invaded their homeland.

Known to history as the "33 Orientals," the rebels, under the leadership of Juan Antonio Lavalleja and Fructuoso Rivera, mounted an impressive revolt. The local population was quick to rally to their standard, and the authorities in Buenos Aires, seeing a chance to incorporate the Banda Oriental into their sphere of influence, sent land and naval forces to help the rebels.

Argentine intervention brought war between

*A painting by Diógenes Hequet in the Uruguayan National Museum of Fine Arts shows Artigas entering Montevideo in 1815, to declare his country's independence.*

Argentina and Brazil, with the Brazilians subjecting Buenos Aires to a tight and effective naval blockade. The blockade put a virtual stop to Great Britain's trade in the area, and British diplomats in 1828 succeeded in negotiating a settlement between the two warring South American rivals. As part of the settlement, it was agreed that Uruguay should be created as a buffer, and from this beginning, Uruguay has maintained its independence ever since, sometimes a precarious freedom.

*The swearing of allegiance by Uruguay's "33 Orientals" (so called because they were from the Banda Oriental) is the subject of this painting.*

*In this scene from the 1865–70 war with Paraguay, the white flag of truce is raised and the fighting stops, while Uruguay's Florida Battalion pays its respects to its commander, who has just fallen in battle.*

## NATIONHOOD

At the time of its creation as a nation, Uruguay's prospects were scarcely promising. It was a nearly empty land with fewer than 100,000 people. Most of these were *gauchos*, who managed the cattle and their domain in a Wild West style, and shepherds, who tended flocks scattered about the nation's grasslands. Only in the capital city was there a group of people with more than the barest essentials of education and culture, and this constituted an unrepresentative élite. Yet it was precisely this group that had to wrestle with the problem of creating a nation.

On July 18, 1830, Uruguay promulgated its Constitution, laying an enlightened documentary basis for a national life. The drafters either did their job exceedingly well, or their successors had neither time nor skill to do better. The Constitution remained in effect for 89 years, a remarkable record considering the frequency with which constitutions were scrapped and rewritten in other South American republics, and with which governments in Uruguay were turned out of office.

One reason for the survival of the Uruguayan Constitution was that it enabled local political

groups to reapportion the spoils of power from time to time, as realignments occurred within the nation's parties, and to revise and modernize public institutions within constitutionally approved norms. In addition, Uruguay's leaders were zealous in protecting the privilege of free speech within the nation's parliament—even when legislators voiced views directly opposed to those of the executive of the moment.

## A NEW TROY

Though for the next 70 years, Uruguay's continued existence was threatened by nearby countries and by internal strife, the nation early adopted a two-party system of politics and government. By 1836, two well defined parties, each with its own private *gaucho* army, had grown up around former leaders of the rebellious Immortal Thirty-Three. Manuel Oribe became the chief of a group of Conservatives, called "Blancos" ("Whites") because of the white ribbons they wore on their hatbands for identification. Their opponents, who wore red ribbons, were the "Colorados" ("Reds"), under the leadership of Fructuoso Rivera.

The rivalry of these two groups, which extends down to the present day, has been

*Even during the period of civil strife in the mid-19th century, Montevideo had, as it has today, a gracious style of life. Seen here is the Plaza Independencia as it looked then.*

periodically complicated by the meddlesome interventions of other nations. In 1843, for example, Manual Rosas, the Argentine dictator, supported one Uruguayan faction at the expense of the other, and thereby helped touch off an 8½-year struggle, known in local history as "The Great War."

The fighting included a protracted Argentine siege of Montevideo, carried out through the intermittent imposition of a naval blockade, and disorganized, though persistent, land assaults. In Paris, the struggle inspired the great writer, Alexandre Dumas, in a book called *Montevideo: A New Troy*, to compare the lot of the Uruguayan capital to that of ancient Troy, laid siege by the Greeks.

Besides becoming the focus of international attention, the war took on the proportions of a civil war in Argentina, even as it had in Uruguay, with the opposing sides either for or against the tyrant Rosas. From Italy came Giuseppe Garibaldi, one of the founders of the modern nation of Italy, to win a hero's laurels for his part in toppling Rosas, in an Argentine uprising in 1851.

With the signing of a peace treaty on October 8, 1851, Uruguay found domestic tranquillity short-lived. Twice during the next 16 years, a Colorado president, General Venancio Flores, had to request Brazilian help to maintain himself in office. In return for this help, Flores committed his nation to join with Argentina and Brazil in their 1865–70 war against heavily armed but hopelessly overpowered Paraguay.

Uruguay's participation in this bitter struggle was minor. No sooner was this conflict over, than Uruguay was torn again by internal strife.

The Colorados easily emerged the winners, and by 1872 it had become apparent that they were strong enough to maintain their hold indefinitely. Widespread acceptance of this fact led both Colorado and Blanco civil and military leaders to strike a deal, under which the Blancos were given control of key public offices, and the local police forces in 4 of the country's departments (provinces), while the Colorados were allowed to dominate the other departments and run the national government. Following a brief uprising in 1897, Blanco control was increased to include 6 departments.

This arrangement provided the basic structure of Uruguay's two-party system, which

*Montevideo in 1900 was a provincial capital, with low buildings and open, tranquil parks. Shown here is the Plaza Constitución.*

If there was a single turning point in Uruguay's struggle for stability, it was perhaps the accord which followed the assassination of President Juan Iriarte Borda in 1897. Iriarte, a Colorado, had dictatorial tendencies—his reliance on the army for support had led to civil war. On his death, leaders of both political parties laid down their arms and signed a political agreement which provided that the political rights of all citizens were to be respected.

The incoming Colorado president made the achievement of domestic peace his highest priority and put an end to the civil strife which had stagnated productivity on the nation's farms.

Uruguayans, who had seen or participated in some 50 revolutions in 70 years, breathed easier. Finally, in the national accord following the death of President Iriarte Borda, there was hope. Besides burying the hatchet, Uruguay's feuding parties had perhaps unwittingly created an atmosphere in which at last the nation's leaders could work toward defining Uruguayan solutions to Uruguayan problems.

## DON PEPE

As the nation faced this improved situation, there appeared on the scene José Batlle Ordoñez ("Batlle" is pronounced "Byé-zhay" by Uruguayans), or "Don Pepe." Son of a former president, Batlle had founded a leading newspaper and after several years' service as a congressman, was elected senator in 1898, and president in 1903.

Armed with a strong personality, new ideas, and a genius for political organization, Batlle led not only a new administration but launched a new era. He served twice as president, 1903–07 and 1911–15, and remained a dominant influence in Uruguayan politics long after his death in 1929.

Batlle based his appeal to the electorate on

through the years has seen the conservative Blanco party dominant among the rural-based rancher class, and the more liberal Colorado party dominant in the cities and drawing particular strength from the capital of Montevideo.

While this workable rearrangement for exercising national and local power was being hammered out, Uruguay itself was changing. In the latter decades of the 19th century, revolutionary violence subsided, and the nation's leaders came to the fore through the more peaceful type of coup d'état. By contrast with the earlier rough-hewn *gaucho caudillos*, Uruguay's presidents and ranking public officials were, more and more, regular army officers, men of some education and refined manners.

During the late 19th century, social and political changes were accelerated by heavy immigration from Europe, particularly from Italy. The immigrants, many of them skilled workers and their families from countries with well defined political traditions, made a marked contribution to Uruguayan life. They demanded improvements in the country's schools, they increased the nation's productivity and they added a fresh measure of social consciousness to both of Uruguay's political parties.

*Named for the man who brought modern social legislation to the nation, Batlle Park in Montevideo contains this stadium, the scene of Uruguay's major soccer matches.*

moral force. He sought and won backing from the nation's forgotten workers, and a then silent middle class—social elements not previously wooed by office seekers.

Under his leadership, armed politics gave way to electoral politics, though not without a fight. The fight was a Blanco rebellion, which started on Christmas Day, 1903, and ended with a rebel defeat on September 1st in the following year. In putting down the insurrection, Batlle exercised firmness and persuasion. In the process, he gave Uruguayans a sense of national morale, a sense of purpose, and the feeling that social progress and a better life for all could be achieved.

Batlle was energetic in the promotion of education, the improvement of conditions among the nation's workers, and increased efficiency in public administration. During his years in office, railways were built, ports modernized, and waterworks, gas, electricity and telephones introduced. He emancipated his country from foreign exploitation, and safeguarded free institutions.

He channelled the currents of reform and change in his time, and gave them sweeping force. At the same time, he held off radical elements who would have had him reform faster, conservatives who wanted no reform at all, and dawdling statesmen who were mainly concerned with pocketing the rewards of office. As a result of his leadership, Uruguay, two generations and more ago, achieved social and economic goals that much of the world today is still far from reaching.

In 1919, under Batlle's influence, a new Constitution became effective. This provided for a popularly elected President, a popularly elected 9-man National Council of Administration, and a two-house Congress, but with a 7-member permanent commission empowered to act while Congress was not in session. The Blancos did not oppose this new Charter seriously. It was hard for them, in a country that was enjoying peace and prosperity, to campaign against social security, workers' rights, and the break-down of class divisions.

Government in accordance with Batlle's

*Presidents of the American republics, including Lyndon B. Johnson (front row, right) met at Uruguay's famous beach resort of Punta del Este in 1967.*

principles worked well enough until the great depression which lasted from 1929 until the mid-1930's. Then the normal procedure of government broke down, and President Gabriel Terra quarrelled with the National Council of Administration and was the object of impeachment proceedings by the Congress. After using force to suppress his opposition, Terra dissolved both the Council and the Congress and for 4 years ruled as a dictator. He persuaded the country to accept a new Constitution in 1934, which provided for a representative and democratic form of government, headed by a President, assisted by a 9-man Council of Government—whose members were appointed by the President, not elected by the people.

This system worked fairly well until the end of 1951, when, in a national plebiscite, the people voted to substitute for the President, a 9-man executive body—the National Council of Government—under which the Presidency rotated from one member to another of the majority party. Under this system, the Blancos, in 1958, won a national election for the first time in 93 years. In 1966, after discovering that the government lacked decisiveness, Uruguayans restored the one-man Presidency, and the Colorados came back to power.

*The Palacio Estevez, on Montevideo's Plaza Independencia, houses the presidential offices. The presidency of Uruguay has undergone a number of changes since the office was first established by the Constitution of 1830. The most recent development took place in 1973, when the army assumed real power in Uruguay and the president became a mere figurehead.*

# 3. GOVERNMENT

THE MODERN structure of Uruguay's government dates from 1967, when a new Constitution was adopted as a means of promoting the progress of a nation which had fallen into dire economic straits. Through their new Constitution, Uruguayan legislators sought to provide for a needed and lacking central executive authority. The old system, a rotating Chief Executive with 9 members of a Council of State serving alternately as the supreme authority, was discarded as unworkable in view of the necessity for firm executive action.

## PRESIDENTIAL SYSTEM

The new Constitution provided once again for a Presidential system, with a President and Vice President who are elected for 5-year terms and whose duties are comparable to those of equivalent officers of the United States government. In Uruguay, the President serves as the supreme authority, and acts with the advice of an 11-member council of ministers.

In performing necessary liaison between the Chief Executive and the nation's legislature,

Uruguayans who have taken an important part in hemisphere affairs include Dr. José A. Mora, former Secretary General of the Organization of American States.

*The entrance hall of Uruguay's Capitol building is rich in ornamentation, including murals depicting the country's history. The hall is called in Spanish the "Salon de los Pasos Perdidos," or "hall of lost steps."*

ministers of the council may attend and speak at sessions of either house of the General Assembly, as the legislature is called, but they may not vote in proceedings there. Under the Uruguayan system, the President may not immediately succeed himself in office—he must await the lapse of 5 years before becoming eligible for a second term.

## THE GENERAL ASSEMBLY

The General Assembly makes the laws of Uruguay. It consists of two houses, the Senate and the Chamber of Representatives. The people elect the 30 members of the Senate at large (without regard to political districts) for 5-year terms.

The Chamber of Deputies, the lower house of Uruguay's legislature, has 99 members or deputies, who are elected according to popula-tion, to represent each of Uruguay's 19 departments.

With legislative salaries generally low, members of both houses of the General Assembly often have another profession. As might be expected, there are frequent conflicts of interests, when legislators representing banking, trade unions, and other groups carry their private interests on over to the floor of the Assembly.

## ELECTIONS

Uruguayan elections are among the most vibrant and complicated on earth. The fact that Uruguayan men and women turn out to vote in such numbers—80 to 90 per cent in recent years—is a tribute not only to their interest in the electoral process, but also to their intelligence, since they are able to fathom a system

*The Senate, the upper house of the General Assembly, is here seen in session.*

whose complexities make an election in the United States seem simple by comparison.

At the general election of 1971, Uruguayan voters on the national level were presented with the opportunity to vote for one among 10 major candidates for the Presidency, the leading one of whom was ineligible for the Presidency. He was running, however, in anticipation of voter approval of a Constitutional amendment put to the voters on the same day as the general election. Had the amendment passed, and it did not, the incumbent President, of the Colorado party, would have been allowed to succeed himself in office.

As matters turned out, the amendment failed and the votes for the incumbent President were transferred to his stand-in at the polls, a man barely known to the Uruguayan electorate. Under the Uruguayan system, what in the United States are considered primary elections are held at the same time as general elections—meaning that each major party goes into the elections with more than one candidate.

In the 1971 elections, the Colorado party offered the voters 6 candidates, the Blanco party, two. Under the Uruguayan system, the eligible candidate who wins the most votes as an individual does not necessarily win. For, in Uruguay, the winner is determined by first adding up the votes of all candidates running under the banner of each party, and then, according the Presidency to the party which racks up a majority of the votes. The individual who is named President is the one who within all of the candidates of the successful party has won the most votes.

To complicate matters further, the voter is entitled to choose one as the President of his choice from a wide field of contenders, but within the party he can vote for the contenders for various offices, according to factions. This means that there are varying combinations of national and local candidates for office. During the 1971 elections, for example, there were more than 200 individual alignments of candidates.

*Uruguayans, wise in the ways of their election system, listen to a 1972 presidential candidate.*

For an outsider, such a system seems unwieldy in the extreme, but the Uruguayan is sophisticated in his country's politics. The 1971 election was a very close one, and it took three months for the Uruguayans to certify a winner —something that kept *politicos* of the nation on the edge of their chairs.

## THE JUDICIAL SYSTEM

Uruguay's Supreme Court consists of a Chief Justice and 4 Associate Justices who serve 10-year terms and are appointed by the nation's General Assembly. Like the President and Vice President, justices of the Supreme Court may not be immediately reappointed to another term of office—they must await the lapse of 5 years.

As in the case of the United States Supreme Court, Uruguay's top court passes on the constitutionality of all laws passed by the federal and local governments. Unlike the U.S. court, it appoints judges for all lower courts and all justices of the peace.

## LOCAL GOVERNMENT

Each of Uruguay's departments has its own departmental council with executive functions, and an assembly with legislative duties. All officers at the departmental and national levels

are elected by the Uruguayan people, with all those over 18 able to vote.

The department of Montevideo has a 65-member assembly and a 7-member council. The other departments have 31-member assemblies and 5-member councils. Smaller towns are governed by a 5-member council appointed by the departmental council, with proportional representation from the nation's political parties.

## POLITICAL PARTIES

The Colorados, with their base in the capital city, generally believe that the government should take an active rôle in the management of the nation and its principal businesses. The Blanco party is the representative of the nation's landed gentry, who stand in opposition to an overly powerful government.

In this, the Blancos seem to have been fighting a losing struggle, since the government has been exercising more and more control over Uruguayan life.

## TUPAMARO TERRORISM

During the 1960's, the Uruguayan government was called upon to confront a serious challenge to law and order, with the emergence of a well organized terrorist movement, the

*"Go home Yankee assassins" says the sign in the middle of the picture. It was painted by members of Uruguay's Socialist Youth Movement ("Juventud Socialista") in 1965, when President Lyndon Johnson sent United States Marines into the Dominican Republic, to help put down disorders there. Note the antique car from the 1920's.*

*Tupamaros*, who take their name from a rebellious Peruvian Inca chieftain of the late 18th century, Tupac Amaru. The Tupamaros, many of them recruited from the sons and daughters of Uruguay's predominant middle class, proved to be a remarkably persistent menace, since they have the support of large numbers of Uruguayans discontented with the nation's economic slide.

Tupamaro tactics have included kidnapping, business and bank hold-ups, and murder—and their activities are splashed on the front pages of newspapers around the world. Among their more prominent actions, the Tupamaros murdered an abducted member of the United States embassy staff, who was advising the Uruguayan government on how to put an end to lawless terrorism. The terrorists also kidnapped the British ambassador, and carried out one of the most successful robberies in Uruguayan history.

## MILITARY TAKEOVER

To put down the political terrorism—which was causing severe problems for the Uruguayan economy—the Uruguayan government substantially increased the size and efficiency of the nation's police and armed forces. Over a 10-year period, increased outlays for the nation's law and order forces paid off in the putting down of Tupamaro terrorism, but they also succeeded in making the military the dominant factor in the nation's government.

In June, 1973, riding high in popular esteem because of their successful actions against the Tupamaros, Uruguay's military leaders closed down the legislature—acting, as they announced at the time, to preserve the nation's new-found domestic tranquillity.

Working through the device of a National Security Council (COSENA), Uruguay's military leaders have since been exercising what

*Uruguay's police and armed forces were substantially increased during the 1960's to counter the rise of terrorism by the Tupamaros.*

amounts to the controlling political influence in the life of the nation. They have succeeded in restoring a needed measure of order to the nation, which over the period of Tupamaro terrorism was plagued with runaway inflation, severe unemployment, and an almost total lack of investor interest. But the nation's military leaders have eclipsed in prominence the nation's elected civilian authorities.

When and whether Uruguay will return to truly representative democratic forms in the foreseeable future remains a large question mark.

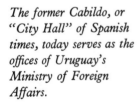

*The former Cabildo, or "City Hall" of Spanish times, today serves as the offices of Uruguay's Ministry of Foreign Affairs.*

*Well fed and well dressed, the people of Montevideo are typical of the middle-class majority in Uruguay.*

# 4. PEOPLE

URUGUAY'S 3,000,000 people are bright and sturdy. They eat more meat than the people of the United States and England. And they are overwhelmingly middle class in economic status and in their basic outlook on life.

The absence of extremes of wealth or poverty makes Uruguay an agreeable country to visit. The average Uruguayan, whether a worker or civil servant, does not have ambitions for his country to obtain greater wealth or influence on the world scene. He is easy to get along with, intelligent, gracious to a fault in his style of living, and dedicated to friends and family.

Though his wife and children have good clothes and good food, the Uruguayan generally does not attach undue importance to material possessions. Few countries in the world have such a sense of human proportion in everything —of such balance and avoidance of extremes.

## IMMIGRATION FROM EUROPE

That Uruguay should have a distinctly European quality is not surprising, for 9 out of every 10 Uruguayans were born in Europe, or had parents or grandparents who were. Almost 90 per cent of the population is of either Spanish or Italian ancestry, in about equal proportions. Because of the high level of Uruguayan life, Italians from cities in the old

A typical "gaucho" wears the traditional baggy black trousers and embroidered shirt. He is well fed, has probably had a good elementary education, is hard-working and knows what he thinks on almost any subject.

French, Germans, Dutch, Greeks, and Scandinavians. The British have been settling in significant numbers since the early 19th century, and the so-called "Anglo-Uruguayan community" exercises a distinct and strong influence in local affairs.

There are few blacks in Uruguay, and these are about evenly divided between town and country. While there is no open discrimination against blacks, few are to be found in the upper ranks of government, business, or the professions.

The country's original inhabitants, the Charrua Indians, have left behind a mere legend of more than a century's resistance to Spanish and Portuguese colonizers. Today, less than 10 per cent of Uruguay's population can trace any aboriginal blood, though this is a cause of family pride.

country have found it easier to become assimilated in Uruguay than have Spaniards, many of whom have immigrated from impoverished rural areas of Spain.

Other European nationalities are represented in the cosmopolitan Uruguayan population, including Portuguese, English, Irish, Welsh,

Though Uruguay has become the home of the sons and daughters of several European

An immigrant from Spain has come to settle in Uruguay, but still wears the beret of the Old World.

*The Jackson Episcopal Church is one of numerous Protestant houses of worship in Montevideo.*

lands, the nation's cultural traditions are Spanish. The universal language is Spanish—or, better said, the distinctively accented Río de la Plata variant of Spanish.

## RELIGION

The majority of Uruguay's people profess affiliation with the Roman Catholic Church, though Uruguayans are the first to say that they are casual about their religion. Protestantism, represented by many denominations and hundreds of congregations long present in Uruguay, has grown markedly in strength and influence in recent years.

Since the Constitution of 1919, Church and State have been separated, though the bond between them was never strong or close, except in early colonial times before the Jesuits were expelled. There is no patron saint, no national shrine of renown, nor any mass pilgrimage. Religious holidays have been secularized— Christmas is "Family Day," and Holy Week "Tourism Week"—a holiday when virtually the entire population takes to the beaches, the hills, or the countryside, and public lodgings and camp grounds are filled to capacity. Politically, the Roman Catholic Church tends to make use of the Christian Democratic Party as a vehicle for voicing its ideas and publicizing its objectives—a party that is relatively insignificant in Uruguay.

*One of the Three Kings greets a young spectator during a Christmas pageant in Montevideo.*

*The Law School is one of the numerous faculties of the University of the Republic in Montevideo.*

## COMMUNICATIONS

Uruguay is well served by communications media. Nearly every Uruguayan listens to one or another of some 70 radio stations in the nation, 30 of them broadcasting from the capital city. About half of the total population is reached by some 15 television stations, 4 of them powerful networks broadcasting from the capital.

Besides Uruguayan radio, the nation is served by stations transmitting from such nearby metropolitan areas as Buenos Aires in Argentina, and Pôrto Alegre and São Paulo in Brazil. Government-run radio stations in Uruguay broadcast much symphonic and classical music, which the public receives enthusiastically—so much so that the government sponsors a national symphony orchestra and ballet company.

Montevideo has 7 daily newspapers, with a combined circulation of approximately 400,000. Of these, *El País* is the organ of the Blanco party; and four other papers, *El Día, El Diario, Acción,* and *La Mañana,* serve the interests of the incumbent Colorado party. It should be noted that besides being heavy consumers of newspapers, Uruguayans are avid readers of books—today's best-sellers circulate in Montevideo practically as soon as they do elsewhere in the world.

## EDUCATION

Uruguayans are a well educated people. As a nation, Uruguay shares with Argentina the laurels for the highest level of educational attainment in Latin America. Uruguay leads all Latin American countries in adult literacy and the proportion of its children in primary school.

Both private and public schools are very good in Uruguay—graduates of either are well read, alert, and some are so imbued with academic tastes that they go on to pursue their intellectual interests over a lifetime. It is not uncommon to find a Uruguayan bank teller, office worker or government employee seriously cultivating some intellectual or artistic hobby or avocation.

It is a tradition in Uruguay that a public education is the birthright of every child. This emphasis dates from the 1870's when a remarkable educator, José Pedro Varela, inspired many young Uruguayans with a desire to become teachers and infused the entire nation with enthusiasm for the development and improvement of the existing educational system. The Ministry of Culture has charge of education and, it is worth noting, has long had cabinet status.

Approximately 90 per cent of all children aged 6 through 8 are in primary schools, and most of them complete 6 grades. High schools are of two kinds. One leads to a diploma known as the *bachillerato,* approximately equivalent to

*The children of Uruguay, including these orphans seen at a party, are well dressed, bright and alert youngsters as a rule.*

*Neatly tilled plots surround the School of Agriculture at Sayago.*

*The School of Medicine in Montevideo embodies the massive, ornate style of the late 19th century.*

*The School of Engineering is housed in one of the more modern buildings at the University of the Republic.*

*The Uruguayan Labor University in Montevideo administers the country's vocational schools.*

the first two years of undergraduate university in the United States. The other offers vocational training in such fields as carpentry, automobile and heavy-machinery mechanics, electricity, radio repair, public health nursing, or hospital administration. In rural areas, vocational schools may teach animal husbandry, soil conservation, or dairying. The vocational training is administered as apart of the Uruguayan Labor University (UTU).

At the top of Uruguay's educational system is the University of the Republic, composed of several colleges—Law and Social Sciences, Medicine, Engineering, Architecture, Chem-

*A sewing class is in progress in one of the schools, the Uruguayan Labor University.*

*A country woman stands before her typical rural dwelling constructed of brick covered over by stucco.*

istry and Pharmacy, Dentistry, Economic Sciences and Administration, Veterinary Medicine, and Humanities and Sciences. There is no central campus, though one is projected for completion before the end of the 1970's. Most university studies cover 6 years and lead to a doctoral degree in a particular field.

The professions have flourished in Uruguay, particularly the practice of medicine. Uruguayan doctors, graduates of the country's medical school and often of some of the best universities of Europe have long had a tradition for providing the country with an outstandingly competent and compassionate service—a system that has reached out to provide for the health of the poorest among the citizenry.

## RURAL LIFE

The people of the Uruguayan countryside are hard-working, thrifty, and dedicated to old-fashioned values. Traditionally, the nation's farms and ranches have provided the conservative Blanco party with its base of strength. In part, this conservatism arises out of a familiar kind of country-versus-city hostility. Uruguayan farmers feel that they generate the income of the nation, which is then spent wastefully by the soft, city-based bureaucracy. In expressing beliefs of this nature, the Uruguayan farmer is well spoken, generally well informed and forthright. By contrast with many of the *campesinos* (farmers) of the

*Like the cowboys of Uruguay's past, this farm worker enjoys chewing tobacco.*

**41**

*In Uruguay's mild climate, country people often go barefoot and live in simple rammed-earth houses. However, they are far from being like the poor peasants of other Latin American countries, for they are literate and very well nourished.*

*A health worker takes leave of a rural family after a visit.*

*In some parts of northern Uruguay, along the border with Brazil, there are rural communities composed of flimsy thatched huts without proper sanitation. In these areas, the government has launched rural health projects with the aid of the World Health Organization (WHO) and the United Nations Children's Fund (UNICEF).*

Andean nations, for example, who scratch out a poverty-level existence from worn-out and rocky soils, the farmer of Uruguay tills and ranches some of the most prosperous lands of South America. He and his family are well fed, often well educated and well dressed; they have the dignity that comes from being productively employed.

## THE GAUCHO

The legendary *gaucho* is an idealized version of the real life *gaucho*, something like the stereotyped screen cowboy of North America's Wild West, portrayed by Hollywood.

Today's *gauchos* wear blue jeans, a topcoat, and soft black hats with the brim upturned in the front. While horseback riding is still a

*A country mother and her son inspect their vegetable garden.*

*It is becoming rare now to see a cowboy dressed in the old style—baggy trousers, poncho, leather boots— and mounted on a saddle of sheepskin.*

popular sport in Uruguay, more likely than not, today's *gaucho* drives a jeep or truck about his work. If he does ride a horse, he probably is mounted on a western-style saddle, rather than the sheepskin of the romantic *gaucho* past. He carries with him a thermos of hot water to make his maté, and a transistor radio. He has added vegetables to his meat-heavy diet.

But, in the national consciousness, the old-time *gaucho*, clad in a long woollen poncho, still rides and fights with his *facon*, or knife, whenever the opportunity presents itself. This image of him was given eternal life, it seems, by

José Hernandez, an Argentine who nearly a century ago wrote the epic poem, *Martín Fierro*. This is as widely read in Uruguay as in Argentina, and has become a part of the national heritage. Uruguayans quote from it as readily as Americans and British quote Shakespeare or the King James Bible.

## WRITERS

During the 19th century, Uruguayans aped European patterns in their literary creations, but in recent years they have turned to their own national literary themes. The precursor of this

*Gauchos in traditional outfits "break" a horse.*

*A couple of guitars, a sunny day, and some "gauchos" are the ingredients of an open-air fiesta in rural Uruguay.*

modern nationalist trend was José Alonso y Trelles (1857–1924), who wrote about *gauchos* and tried to reproduce their dialect. The most important and influential Uruguayan writer is José Enrique Rodo (1872–1917), widely known and admired for his philsophical essay, *Ariel*. While this deals with the interaction between reason and spirit, it has been widely interpreted as symbolizing the struggle and conflict between a rich and materialistic United States and a poor but struggling and idealistic Latin America. It is often quoted by those who would downgrade and criticize the United States, justly or not.

Outstanding among Uruguay's poets is Juan Zorrilla de San Martín (died 1931), whose epic poem, *Tabaré*, is an allegory depicting the victory of the human spirit, symbolized by the Spaniard, over the forces of nature, symbolized by the primitive Charrua. Two women poets have achieved recognition— Juana de Ibarbourou, who wrote of the parallel between the seasons of the year and those of man's earthly life; and Delmira Augustini, who has written of the ecstasies of physical love.

## MUSIC AND ART

Music has not been as highly developed as literature. Much Uruguayan folk music, which has been making a comeback in recent decades, has as its theme *gaucho* legends. The most

typical folk dance is the *pericón*, danced by couples. The tango, which flourished from the 1920's through the 1950's, has been losing out against the competition of various popular music fads that emanate from Brazil, New York, Liverpool and London.

Serious music, though it is played and enjoyed a great deal, has not been cultivated much by Uruguayans. An exception to the rule is Hector Tosar Errecart, born in 1923, a Uruguayan pianist and composer of some note.

Uruguay's first prominent painter was Juan Manuel Blanes (1830–1901), who gained fame for his paintings illustrating the nation's history. Prominent artists at work in Uruguay in recent years include the painter José Cuneo, born in 1887, and the sculptor José L. Zorrilla de San Martín, born 1891. The Uruguayan sculptor José Belloni, whose works grace Montevideo's parks, is well known for his depiction of the ox-drawn, high-wheeled *pampas* cart, the *carreta*.

Undoubtedly the best known contemporary artist is Carlos Paez Vilaró, known in the United States for the 536-foot-long (161 metres) mural in the Pan American Union building in Washington, D.C. Paez is an all-round artist— he writes poetry and sculpts in addition to painting. His work in progress is a fantastic structure that is both a sculpture and a house at Punta del Este. He is both building and living in

*Uruguay's leading theatre, the Teatro Solís, is located in the heart of downtown Montevideo, close to restaurants, hotels, and a beautiful open park.*

*The government runs the gambling casinos in Uruguay, which are frequented by average middle-class people, many of them making small bets.*

*The beach at Pocitos, one of the wealthier suburbs of the capital, is crowded almost any weekend during good weather.*

it at the same time and it has received critical praise at home and abroad.

## RECREATION

Montevideo offers year-round theatre, opera and ballet performances, as well as a great many sporting events. Horsemanship is a tradition in Uruguay and horse racing, rodeos, horse shows and polo (introduced by the English immigrants) are very popular. Boating, swimming

*Uruguayans are fanatics when it comes to "fútbol." Whole families are to be found in the stands at important matches. The flag seen here is the pennant of the Peñarol team, and has yellow and black horizontal bars and 11 stars—one for each player.*

*Children in a school pageant in Montevideo dress in the costumes of many countries to symbolize the United Nations Children's Fund (UNICEF).*

*This woman, mother of a farm family, brews her "maté" on the spot. At the base of her silver "bombilla" is an enlarged perforated compartment in which the maté leaves are placed. Then she pours hot water from a vacuum bottle into the gourd holding the "bombilla."*

holiday before the beginning of Lent, but in Montevideo the festival assumes dazzling proportions, rivalling the famous Carnival of Rio de Janeiro in Brazil.

## FOOD

As might be expected, European influences are strong in the restaurants of Montevideo, many of which serve Italian and French cuisine. Typically Uruguayan dishes, like those of Argentina, reflect the country's gaucho past and meat-eating tastes. Especially popular is *asado*, a sort of barbecue of beef or lamb, rubbed with coarse salt and roasted on a spit over hot coals. A switch on this is *asado con cuero*, yearling beef roasted in its own hide.

Other meat dishes are *parrillada*, a mixed grill of sausages, kidneys and liver, and *punchero*, a dish of meat boiled together with chick peas, bacon and various vegetables. Popular as snacks or as appetizers are *empanadas*, little spiced meat pies. Coffee, tea, wine and beer are consumed, but the national drink is *maté*, a tea brewed from a species of native holly. Among farmers and ranchers, it is customary to drink *maté* from a gourd, with a silver tube called a *bombilla*.

and other water sports have thousands of participants, as have tennis, golf and basketball.

However, by far the most popular sport in this sports-conscious country is *fútbol* (football) or soccer. The two chief soccer clubs, the "Peñarol" and the "Nacional," have followings as devoted as any in the world.

All of Uruguay celebrates Carnival, the 3-day

*Young city dwellers take a "maté" break on a Montevideo beach.*

A new plant for the treatment of water provides Montevideans with fresh and pure drinking water.

The Agricultural Research Station at La Estanzuela carries out studies on crops and livestock.

At La Estanzuela, plant geneticists cross-pollinate sorghum, a cereal grass somewhat similar to maize.

*Beef accounts for about 75 per cent of Uruguay's meat production, the remainder consisting of lamb, mutton and pork.*

# 5. ECONOMY

AGRICULTURE is the mainstay of the Uruguayan economy. Meat sales alone account for almost half of the nation's export earnings, and wool sales from one quarter to one third of the total.

Most of the other items that figure importantly in Uruguay's income from overseas—hides, maize, wheat, citrus fruits, barley, rice, oats, sugar, tobacco and linseed oil—are products of the land. The nation is making a firm effort to develop its manufacturing capacity, however, and now exports such items as textiles, cement, wines and an increasingly expanding line of processed foods.

Uruguay's most important customers are the nations of the European Common Market. In recent years, West Germany has been Uruguay's largest single trading partner, with Brazil second, Italy third, and the United States fourth.

The dominant economic activities in Uruguay are livestock raising and farming. Some 85 per cent of the nation's total farming lands are devoted to raising animals, and the fortunes of the Uruguayan economy rise and fall with the fluctuations of world prices for meat and wool.

Uruguayans are very personally involved in

*Experts from the United Nations Food and Agriculture Organization (FAO) are working with Uruguayan researchers on improved seed production in order to raise the quality of food and forage crops. An FAO expert (right), with his Uruguayan assistants, observes the operation of the blower system used to dry seeds in the processing plant at La Estanzuela.*

*Probably nothing more truly exemplifies the Uruguayan economy than this scene, an inspector marking the grade of beef on a carcass hanging in a refrigeration plant.*

*The Rubino Institute at Pando carries out research on diseases of livestock in an effort to raise the quality of meat production.*

Workers classify different species of maize grown on an experimental farm.

Engineers of the Merín Basin Project study a water-level chart.

A modern harvesting machine is tried out at the Merín Basin Project.

*Sorghum is a valuable fodder crop. Here a worker measures the growth of the maize-like grain in an experimental plot—he is using a surveyor's rod.*

*A Dutch irrigation expert (middle rear) from the United Nation's Food and Agriculture Organization directs the installation of an irrigation pump in the Merín Basin Project.*

this phenomenon. When beef prices are good, or when the nation's treasury is depleted, Uruguayans are asked by their government to eat less beef, so that more of the nation's production can be sold overseas. During these periods, called *vedas*, when it is forbidden to sell beef in public places, Uruguayans must settle for such substitutes as lamb, liver and sausage.

## INCOME

The average Uruguayan earns close to U.S. $1,000 a year, putting the nation in third place among Latin American nations in per capita income, after Argentina and Venezuela. Precise studies of just how fairly Uruguay's income is distributed remain to be made. It is evident, however, to the casual visitor that in Uruguay national earnings are more evenly divided among the general populace than they are in such nations as Argentina, which has a large and en-

trenched wealthy aristocracy, or Venezuela, where the profits from the all-important oil industry line the pockets of the few.

Another reason for the impression of equality is the fact that the Uruguayan government, as part of the drive to create a welfare state, attends to so many citizen needs. Bus fares, subsidized by the government, are incredibly low, amounting to a few pennies for rides of several miles. Health and retirement benefits are provided, again courtesy of a benevolent—some say too benevolent—government.

## GOVERNMENT—A BIG EMPLOYER

The Uruguayan government itself employs approximately one third of the nation's total work force, either directly or indirectly. To the normal staffs of government ministries must be added those of the numerous public corporations and decentralized services. A Uruguayan says:

In an attempt to provide every citizen with a decent home, the Uruguayan government is relying on the latest techniques for building prefabricated housing units.

The Uruguayan government has attempted over the years to provide the finest in medical care for the nation's citizens. Among the best known medical facilities is the Hospital de Clinicas in Montevideo.

"If it's not profitable, you can bet that the government is running it."

Over the years, this philosophy has led to the government's acquisition of the railways, and the electric power, meat packing, petroleum, alcohol, and fisheries industries—among others. Most of these government-run businesses are hopelessly overstaffed, and forced to offer

Because it has a relatively stable population, Uruguay is able to keep up with the construction of new housing. These modern units are being built on the outskirts of Montevideo.

*The National Meat-Packing Plant, once a vital element of Uruguay's economy, has been shut down in recent years owing to trade union trouble—and the inability of the Uruguayan government to run it efficiently.*

services or products at uneconomically low rates. Uruguay's national airline, which has but a single airplane, has more than 1,000 employees.

In addition, there are numerous government-subsidized boards and commissions, many of them with overlapping authority, to control rents and prices, to oversee the nation's tourism business and even operate hotels and run gambling casinos—all with legions of employees. In Uruguay, the theory seems to be that the government must provide a job for every man, even when there is not a job.

*Though Uruguay has no petroleum of its own, it does have a small refinery which, with recent improvements, is able to refine crude oil, bottle butane and propane gas, and produce a modest amount of asphalt.*

*Bars of soap move along the assembly line of a new plant, part of the Uruguayan government's effort to supply more of the domestic needs.*

The worker and his job are stringently protected by a benevolent government. Uruguay has one of the most elaborate codes for civil service of any nation on earth. Government employees enjoy tenure—they can be discharged only for the most shocking derelictions of duty, and not for mere incompetence or inefficiency. The government's retirement system extends to an incredible number of Uruguayans, the rule in the capital city seeming to be that everyone can qualify for a pension, either in his own right or because some relative was once on the government rolls.

*A dockworker at the port of Montevideo heads for home, walking through the arcade of a government building.*

*In a nation with a strong trade union movement, vocational training is of great importance. Here experts explain the wiring of an electric motor to students in one of the trade schools of the Uruguayan Labor University in Montevideo.*

To be fair, it should be emphasized that Uruguayans themselves are the first to criticize the shortcomings of their system; they put up with it because it is democratic. Owing to the importance of government as an employer and to a well developed patronage system, Uruguayans are an intensely political people, zealous in making sure that a fair proportion of their friends and relatives are on the federal payroll.

## TRADE UNIONS

Uruguay's unions, dating from the 1890's, are strong and well organized, and they make their weight felt in the nation's political affairs. The unions were early given a strong boost during the administrations of José Batlle Ordoñez (1903–07 and 1911–15), founder of Uruguay's modern welfare state. Dating from the Batlle era, organized workers in Uruguay have been the beneficiaries of wide-ranging social legislation—a fact that has contributed to Uruguay's emergence as a predominantly middle-class nation.

In 1940, the General Workers Union (UGT) was established, its membership mainly in the construction, textile, maritime, trans-

*Workmen rush to completion the new water purification and sewage treatment plant in Montevideo, built to provide the city with water that can be drunk from the tap without worry.*

*Some of Uruguay's vast wool production goes into making rugs of high quality. This woman is learning the trade at the Labor University.*

*"This factory has been expanded with the help of the Inter-American Development Bank," says the sign in back of the speaker, on the day the improvements to the plant were inaugurated.*

*The Uruguayan government provides training in technical skills such as operating machine tools.*

highest priorities the "democratization" of trade unions, and sought through registration to bring the unions under government control. One reason for this is that since the 1960's, the unions, heavily leftish, have contributed to chaotic conditions in Uruguay's economy, by calling some 700 strikes per year, not to mention even more numerous informal work stoppages.

In general, pressures on workers to apply themselves diligently are not great. Most government employees, for example, work only half a day. In the summer they work in the mornings so as to have the afternoons free for the beach, and in the winter it is the other way round—they work in the afternoons in order to be able to spend the chilly mornings by the fireside at home. Almost all workers—office as well as factory, private as well as government— have a tea-break in the afternoon, with lengthy discussions on all manner of topics and a great deal of personal gossip thrown in.

portation, and service industries. In 1959, UGT's open announcement that it was Communist-led and oriented, provoked something of a split in the Uruguayan trade union movement.

The Communist-dominated National Workers Convention (CNT) is today the largest trade union organization, in a country which has nearly 400,000 union members. These include members of professions that are not unionized in many nations—tellers in banks, for example.

In recent times, Uruguay's military-influenced government has adopted as one of its

## FARM WORKERS

The constrast between the work habits of Uruguay's urban, unionized workers and the nation's farm workers is very great. Industrious and intelligent, Uruguay's farm force compares

*Uruguay's cattlemen are often big businessmen, some of them, like this rancher, owning large herds worth vast sums.*

*Farm workers pour fertilizer into a hopper before spreading it over a field seeded with white clover. Fertilizer, which is essential to produce high-yielding crops, is an important item in Uruguay's farm improvement schemes.*

well with that of any other nation of the western hemisphere.

The nation's livestock is extremely well cared for, as are the fields and pastures which produce more than two thirds of Uruguay's income, yet employ only one fifth of the total number of workers. A visit to a Uruguayan *estancia*, or large farm, is a memorable experience—the work of the place is well organized, well supervised, and well carried out.

Though much of Uruguay's farming is in the hands of a relatively few members of the landowning class, there is little of the feudalism, the

*Wool for foreign markets is carefully baled and loaded for shipment overseas. This particular cargo is headed for Boston, in the United States.*

*Much of rural Uruguay is comprised of level or rolling lands, with good roads for local traffic.*

virtual serfdom, found elsewhere in Latin America, in the raising of such back-breaking crops as sugar cane or coffee. Producers of highly valuable and nutritious beef, Uruguay's farm population takes pride in its work.

## TRANSPORTATION

Uruguay's most important highway leads west out of Montevideo to Colonia, on the Río de la Plata, before swinging west and north to pass Mercedes, a major market city and Fray Bentos, hub of the meat packing industry. It then goes on to Paysandú, head of navigation on the Uruguay River for ocean-going ships, Salto, head of navigation for coastal shipping, and eventually to Artigas on the Brazilian border. In the other direction from Montevideo, to the east, there is a good highway that leads to the Brazilian border at a town called Chuy.

This highway, taken together with the section of the highway leading west out of Montevideo and linking the nation with Buenos Aires, the Argentine capital, is fast becoming a major commercial artery. It is part of the most heavily travelled land route on the east coast of South America, a highway that links 6 major cities—

*The ship alongside the dock in Montevideo carries passengers overnight to Buenos Aires, the capital of Argentina.*

*Surveyors work from a bridge over the Olivar River in eastern Uruguay.*

Rio de Janeiro, São Paulo, Curitiba, Pôrto Alegre, Montevideo, and Buenos Aires.

First class buses keep to split-second schedules along this 1,000-mile-long run (1,600 km.) from Rio de Janeiro to Buenos Aires, as do big semi-trailers carrying products to and from the major urban market places. This east coast corridor has provided Uruguay with a major opening for trade and commerce with the adjoining South American countries.

From Montevideo, there have long been good roads leading into the interior of the country, carrying farm produce and livestock to capital markets. One of these roads runs due north from the capital, passing through the sizable towns of Florida, Durazno, Paso de los Toros, and Tacuarembo, before reaching the Brazilian frontier at Rivera. Another swings northwest from the capital, linking up several agricultural towns before running north near the Argentine border through Paysandú, Salto, and Bella Unión.

*With the help of the Inter-American Development Bank, several thousand miles of new roads have been built, or improved.*

63

# INDEX